A GIFT FOR:

FROM:

DATE:

FOREWORD

I first heard this song about four years ago and I immediately fell in love with it. I was genuinely moved. Craig, KK, and Tim have found a way to take the oldest of stories, the birth of baby Jesus, and make it relevant to us today, with the hope and optimism that defines Christmas. I am so thankful and fortunate to have been given the opportunity to record the song for my Christmas album, because a baby did, and does, really change everything.

—*Faith Hill*

The man she loves
she never touched
How will she keep
his trust?

A baby changes
everything
A baby changes everything

And she cries...

Be not afraid. You are

never

CHRISTMAS AND THE *gift* OF CHRISTMAS

IS YOUR REMINDER THAT YOU ARE

NOT ALONE . . .

YOU ARE NEVER ALONE.

alone,

You have angels.

A BABY CHANGES EVERYTHING.

Rejoice…the Lord is with you…

— Luke 1:28

look

See the world with new eyes.

It's hard to judge others when you are

preoccupied with love.

A baby changes everything.

dreams

A DREAM IS WHAT MIGHT BE.

Even if they've faded, this Gift of Christmas
will breathe new life into them.

To have a baby is to dream new dreams,
to dream further into the future than you ever have before.
This child will change who you are and who you will become.
From the first cry, your dreams will never be the same.

A baby is a dream come true.

She has to leave, go far away

Heaven knows she can't stay

A baby changes everything

lighten up

Nobody's perfect
when they have a baby.

A baby turns every parent into an improv artist
doing the best they can with what they've got.
Luckily, babies don't know if you're "doing it right."

Babies just know if you love them.

Forget the mistakes.
Try again.

Life's like that, too.

Tears dry. Hurts heal.

We live and learn . . .

A baby changes everything.

plans

A baby is upsetting.

What doesn't it upset?

SCHEDULES,

STOMACHS,

HOUSEHOLDS,

  THE BEST LAID PLANS...

LIFE.

But for crying out loud, *it's a baby!*
Who cares!

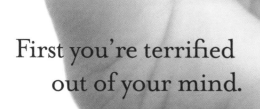

First you're terrified
out of your mind.

Then you're thrilled.

And then it starts to sink in.

now?

You wonder how you got here . . . and where you'll go from here.

You think you can handle it. A baby is so small, after all.

There's nothing to be afraid of. Is there?

All the changes will be okay, right?

Nothing too drastic, right?

Nothing too fast, nothing too scary, nothing too . . . wheeeeee!

A baby changes everything.

She can tell
it's coming soon
But there's no place,
there's no room
A baby
changes everything
A baby changes everything

And she cries...

soon

No matter how ready
(*or not*)
you *think* you are, *nobody is.*

Everyone thinks they know
what will change when the
baby comes. Nobody does.

Everyone thinks
they know a baby changes
everything.

But they don't...
until it does.

Joy to the World!

A baby changes

joy

Behold, I bring
you good tidings
of great joy...
—Luke 2:14

A baby changes

hope

The light
shines in
the darkness…
—John 1:5

A baby changes

love

For God
so loved
the world…
—John 3:16

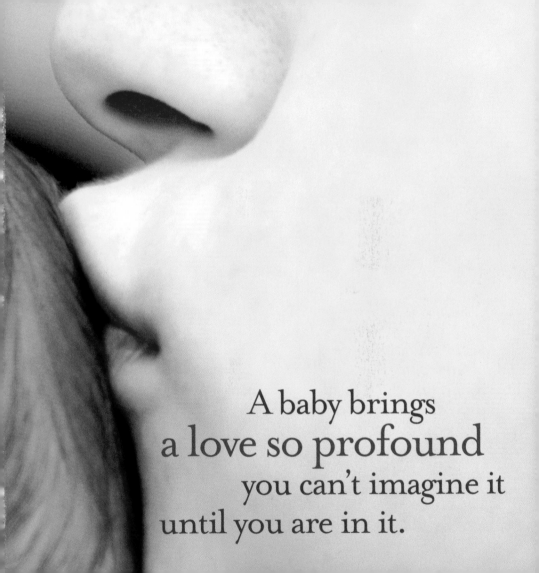

A baby brings
a love so profound
you can't imagine it
until you are in it.

The star . . .
went before them.
—Matthew 2:9

star

Starlight.

The sign.

This baby is special.

This is your baby.

What is the light that lights up your life?

What *light* do you follow?
What *light* do you seek?

What light seeks you?
A baby changes everything.

angels

You can't have a baby alone.

No matter what your situation.
If you have a baby, you are going to need help...

Fortunately,
God has a way of sending
just the right help
at just the right moment.

A baby comes with angels.

A baby changes everything.

Behold.

A baby.
Your baby.
The Baby.

Redemption…fresh start…new hope…

Go on, let it all out…let it all in.
It's Christmas.

And a baby *changes everything.*

*She brought forth
her firstborn Son,
and wrapped Him
in swaddling cloths,
and laid Him
in a manger…*
—Luke 2:7

My whole life was
turned around
I was lost
but now I'm found
A baby changes
everything

grace

Amazing
is the grace
that comes to find you
as gently as a newborn babe.

how sweet the sound…I once was lost…but now I'm found…

The Story Behind

A Baby Changes Everything

Ultimately, this song began with one tiny baby more than two thousand years ago. And a lot of fantastic things have happened as a result. No surprise though—a baby does change everything.

The journey began with KK writing a sermon which led to Craig and Tim writing a song, which then led to all three of us writing this book.

Not long after we wrote the song, we got the news that Faith Hill wanted to record it for her album *Fireflies*. Needless to say, we were thrilled, and we couldn't wait to hear her sing it. However, the long wait for this "baby" to be born had only just begun.

First, Faith told us she loved the song so much she didn't want it to get lost on an album. Instead, she wanted to wait and put it on her very first Christmas album. Of course we said we would wait—we had faith...and Faith...and faith in Faith. But then *Fireflies* did really well and the record label pushed back the Christmas album a year. And then her tour went really well, and the album got pushed back another year.

But finally, it happened. Faith went into the studio and out came a miracle. The wait was worth it—more than worth it.

We hope the song brings you "glad tidings of great joy." It is a special song to us. Craig and Tim are thrilled to get the opportunity to follow up their Grammy-winning Tim McGraw hit, "Live Like You Were Dying" with a Faith Hill song that also celebrates life (the two songs make a nice set). And for KK and Craig, this is their first writing collaboration in fifteen years of marriage (…changes everything).

The song itself is special, but the rest of the story is extraordinary. Many great writers have told it before—Matthew, Mark, and Luke are some of our favorites. Check 'em out!

Merry Christmas,

Craig, KK & Tim

Faith Hill

Since her debut single, "Wild One," held the number-one spot on Billboard's country

singles chart for four weeks in 1994, Faith Hill has gone on to win five Grammys, four

American Music Awards, three CMAs, and

twelve Academy of Country Music awards.

With hits like "The Way You Love Me,"

"Breathe," "This Kiss," and "Cry," Faith

has become one of the most successful and

recognizable stars in country music. She

is married to fellow country superstar Tim

McGraw; the couple have three daughters. This year, Faith releases a much anticipated

Christmas album, Joy to the World, featuring "A Baby Changes Everything" written by

Tim Nichols, Craig Wiseman, and KK Wiseman.